Malaysian Flowers in Colour

Bunga Raya, HIBISCUS, *Hibiscus rosa-sinensis,* Malaysia's national flower.

Malaysian Flowers in Colour

Photography and Text

by

CHIN HOONG FONG
M. AGR. SC., PH. D. (MELB.), M.I. BIOL.

ASSOCIATE PROFESSOR
AGRONOMY AND HORTICULTURE DEPARTMENT
UNIVERSITI PERTANIAN MALAYSIA

TROPICAL PRESS SDN. BHD.
56–2 JALAN MAAROF, BANGSAR BARU
59100 KUALA LUMPUR
MALAYSIA

First published 1977
Ninth impression 1993

ISBN 967–73–0018–0

TYPESETTING, COLOUR SEPARATION,
PRINTED AND BOUND BY ART PRINTING WORKS SDN. BHD.
29 JALAN RIONG, 59100 KUALA LUMPUR
MALAYSIA

Dedicated to
my Mother

Foreword

Malaysia is well known for her rich and varied flora. Although a large proportion are timber species, there are nevertheless a good number of tropical flowering species. Of particular importance amongst these are the orchids which are not only numerous in the wild state but are also widely found in cultivation and they form the nucleus of a multi-million dollar enterprise for the country.

Apart from this native flora, there are many plants which have been introduced from other parts of the world. This has contributed to the diversity of plant life in Malaysia.

In this book a selection of these beautiful flowers to be seen in the Malaysian garden are captured in full colour. It is the first occasion that such a book has been published locally. It is the work of an amateur photographer using a minimum of equipment—just a single reflex lens camera with a 50 mm lens. It awakens us to the floral beauty that is so often unseen in the bustle of our daily lives.

Since Independence, Malaysia has developed tremendously. With urbanization, several new towns, suburbs and housing estates have sprung up. People are becoming conscious of the need to beautify their homes and surroundings. At the same time there is a growing public awareness on the needs to preserve the environment and prevent the spread of pollution. As a result there is an increasing interest in the planting of flowering shrubs and trees.

It is timely then that a book of this type be produced. All the photographs are in colour. A brief description of each plant is given together with the method of propagation. In addition, there is an extended chapter devoted to plant propagation and maintenance, which will assist the enthusiast to establish a garden. This is a book suitable for a wide range of people—for students and naturalists, for gardeners and nurserymen and visitors from overseas.

Tan Sri Datuk Prof. Dr. Mohd. Rashdan bin Haji Baba
Vice Chancellor
Universiti Pertanian Malaysia.

Preface

IN many parts of the world spring comes but once a year, the plants are at the peak of their activities with full blooms to attract the birds and the bees. This activity is actually a way to propagate themselves. But in the tropics, we have the advantage of favourable growing seasons all year round and hence some plants flower all the year round while others are seasonal. Because of the free flowering throughout the year, familiarity has bred contempt. Furthermore, it may be because our flowering trees are mostly evergreen thus lessening their impact on the eyes as compared to the temperate species, such as the cherry blossoms, which are leafless at spring time with only the masses of colourful flowers on the trees to catch our eyes. Also in these days of keeping up with the rat race, everyone is dashing around in his car and does not stop to have a closer look at the local flowers along the highways.

In this book it is my aim to bring to you the most common and some rare, beautiful flowers that you can find growing in our public gardens, homes and wild species along the roadside or highways throughout the country. Over a hundred close-up studies of flowers in colour will provide you with an opportunity to have a closer look at the flowers at your leisure especially those high up on the trees, which are too high to be seen clearly without straining your neck.

The collection of flowers assembled here consists not only of plants that are indigenous to Malaysia, but includes many species which are introduced from other tropical countries. Even the temperate species are included as they thrive well in our highland regions in Cameron and Genting. Since it is the flowers which attract us most by their colours and shapes, the emphasis here is entirely given to the flowers. The selection of these flowers is firstly based on their attractiveness and secondly on their availability throughout the country but not necessarily throughout the year.

Once you have glanced through these colour plates and if you are attracted to their beauty which you have missed out all these years, you may like to get further details of their common name, botanical name, habitat and habit of the plant such as its height, time of flowering, size of flowers, whether it is lasting and whether it is scented. All these details are given very briefly. I hope this book will stimulate you to choose and plant these local species in your own garden or suggest these to be planted in gardens near the vicinity of your home.

A number of books have been written on the flora of Malaysia. These are complete works with detailed descriptions and are illustrated by drawing, or black and white plates, sometimes accompanied with a few colour plates. This is the first time a book on Malaysian flowers is published in full colour. I strongly believe the Chinese saying "A picture is worth a thousand words", especially a colour photograph. This is particularly true for the layman and those who have not much time to spare. This simple book contains the minimum description but it is hoped that the collection of colour photographs will be useful to the home gardeners, nurserymen, overseas visitors and students who wish to learn a little more about our common Malaysian flowers.

The flowers in this collection are arranged in groups according to the habit of the plants. These are the trees, shrubs, climbers, herbs, pot plants, aquatic plants and orchids. Every species described bears the common names, botanical names and also the family to which it belongs. The common names are in the Malaysian and English Language followed by the botanical name. The final section is specially devoted to the propagation, planting and maintenance of plants, so that the reader can grow some of the colourful blooms in his or her own garden. Index to both the common and scientific names are given.

I wish to gratefully acknowledge the Vice Chancellor of the University of Agriculture, Tan Sri Professor Mohd. Rashdan bin Haji Baba for his encouragement and permission to publish this book, Prof. Enoch and Dr. H.S. Yong for their comments, Mr. C.H. Ong for collecting and locating the plants and finally my wife Annie for reading the manuscript and her patience in our photography outings.

CHIN HOONG FONG

May, 1976

Contents

f all flowers
Methinks a rose is best
     Why gentle madam?
It is the very embleme of a maide
For when the west wind courts her gently,
How modestly she blows, and paints the sun,
With her chaste blushes.

SHAKESPEARE

Flowers Bring Peace

Flowers bring peace into a room.
A posy or a single bloom—can dispel a restless
mood.
An atmosphere of quietude—haunts the place
where flowers are.
You forget the things that jar.
So still they stand in vase or bowl.
Their silence speaks unto the soul.
Day by day now autumn comes—beautiful
chrysanthemums—bring proud summer to its close.
Heedless of the fading rose—rich and deep their
colours blaze.
Season of the mellow days—as chrysanthemums
unfold—wine and amber, bronze and gold.
From a blue jug by my chair—they watch me
and I am aware—of their beauty blessing me—
with their own tranquility.
Who comes within this calming spell—
cannot doubt that all is well.

PATIENCE STRONG

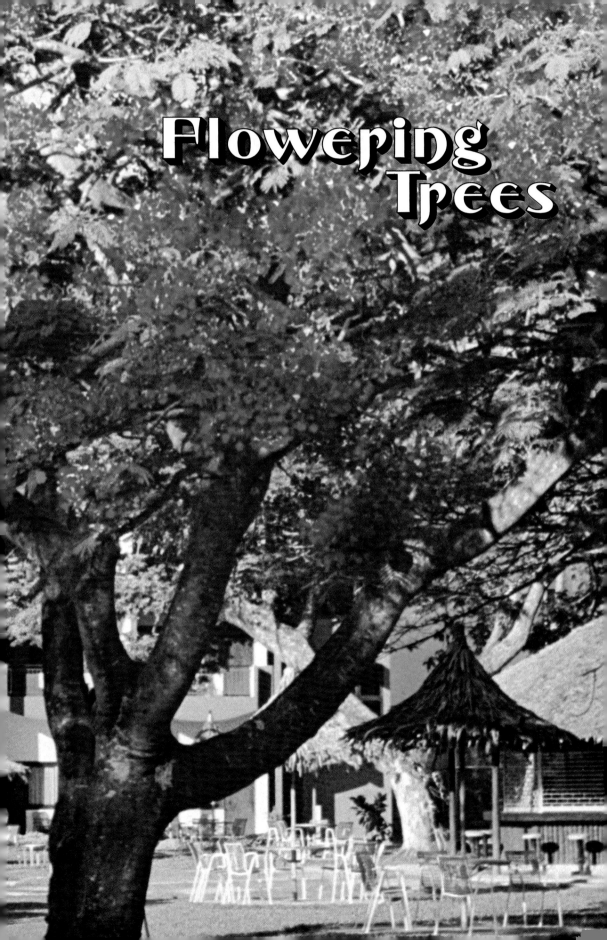

Flowering Trees

Flowering Trees

*M*any a tree is found in the wood,

And every tree for its use is good,

Some for the strength of the gnarled root,

Some for the sweetness of flowers or fruit.

Henry Van Dyke,
Salute the Trees.

MALAYSIA has a very rich flora. Today many introduced and local trees form the backbone of the landscape of our local gardens and countrysides. In this country there is tremendous diversity in plant species varying in colour, texture and density of leaves. Trees themselves differ greatly in sizes and shapes, thus providing a large array of uses. Trees can be used as a screen, for shade and for their flowers.

Tropical trees are mainly evergreen with a few deciduous species. These evergreens produce masses of foliage and the flowers may be as impressive as the cherry blossoms of the temperate regions. Indeed some trees may be even superior to the cherry blossoms in that they bloom several times a year. They are the famous Flame of the Forest *Delonix regia*, and Angsana *Pterocarpus indicus* and Dadap or Coral Tree *Erythrina indica*, which bloom magnificently providing masses of brilliant colours. In contrast to these are the Casuarina, *Casuarina sumatrana* and Ketapang *Terminalia catappa* which are grown for their foliage and shapes.

In this book eighteen trees are selected. All of them produce flowers seasonally, some are more impressive and attractive than others. Although seasonal, some have a few flowering periods in a year. Others produce fragrant flowers. The selection of trees for planting depends on the use i.e. as shade trees, screen or for the avenues. Secondly it depends on the size of the garden. Good examples of flowering shade trees are Angsana and the Yellow Flame *Peltophorum pterocarpum*. Both produce bright attractive yellow flowers regularly and possess sprawling branches thus giving a large canopy. One of the best local trees for a tall screen is Tembusu *Fagraea fragrans*. It has a solid mass of small foliage and annually bears fragrant flowers and bright red berries. Another highly recommended native plant is Ceylon Ironwood *Mesua ferrea*, which grows slowly into a symmetrical cone with pinkish young leaves at the tips of branches. Periodically they produce large, white fragrant flowers. Some trees are planted mainly to add colour to the landscape. Outstanding examples of these are the Flame of the Forest, Dadap and Indian Laburnum *Cassia fistula*. During the flowering seasons, the trees are almost bare. The scarlet flowers of the Flame of the Forest needs no description and the pendulous groups of large yellow flowers of the Indian Laburnum are the most beautiful sight in the full morning sun. These plants are particularly handsome in the northern states of Malaysia as in Penang and they are well worth planting in the garden or along avenues. For the average home garden with limited space, several small trees up to a height of 20 feet are available. These are the attractive Jacaranda *Jacaranda ovalifolia* with its blue mauve flowers, Bauhinia *Bauhinia purpurea* with rose mauve flowers and the Rose of India *Lagerstroemia flos-reginae* which is one of the finest flowering trees in the north with pinkish mauve flowers.

Flowering trees can be propagated either from seeds or by vegetative means. Most of them are easily established from seeds. However, some produce seeds very sparingly and special vegetative propagation techniques have to be adopted. For example, in the case of *Amherstia nobilis* successful propagation can only be achieved by marcotting and even then there is great difficulty. In contrast, Dadap and Angsana are easily propagated by large woody cuttings. All these propagation techniques will be described in detail at the end of this book under *Propagation, Planting and Maintenance of Plants*. In the propagation of plants by seeds, normally a seed is sown in a pot or plastic bag containing garden soil. Seedlings when they have reached a height of 18 inches or more can be transplanted into the ground. It has to be planted correctly in a planting hole to be sited in a suitable place. Usually trees are planted near the borders and background of gardens. Care must be taken to avoid planting too close to a hedge or house as roots from the trees interfere with the growth of hedges or may damage the house. After choosing the correct site, a planting hole 4 feet square and 3 feet deep is dug. Good garden soil together with fertilizer and compost are incorporated and well mixed. After a seedling is planted it is necessary to tie it to a strong stake to keep it upright. The general maintenance of plants will also be described at the end of the book.

Pride of Burma, Amherstia
Amherstia nobilis
LEGUMINOSAE

A beautiful ornamental tree introduced from Burma, about 30 feet in height, is rarely found in gardens. Growth is slow and propagation by means of marcot is often difficult. Flowering is seasonal and the flowers are of delicate pink with patches of yellow on their petals. Requiring a moist climate, it thrives in lowland area with a deep rich well drained soil.

Purple Bauhinia
Bauhinia purpurea
LEGUMINOSAE

A fairly small tree from India and South China, reaching up to 20 feet high. The leaves are blunt and divided into lobes. The flowers are pink to deep rose pink with white streaks on the sides of the odd petal. An ornamental tree, it is propagated by woody cuttings and seeds. Bauhinia looks beautiful when grown individually in a small garden.

**Indian Laburnum,
Golden Shower, Bereksa**
Cassia fistula
LEGUMINOSAE

A deciduous tree, 30 feet high, from India, it grows slowly at its early stages of growth but vigorously once it is established. It requires a sunny place and thrives best in well drained soil. Flowering is seasonal and normally after several years old. At full bloom, the tree is often covered with large pendulous groups of golden yellow flowers. Seeds and marcots (normally large branches) are its means of propagation.

Flame of the Forest, Flamboyant, Gul Mohr, Sepanggil
Delonix regia
LEGUMINOSAE

A native of Madagascar, it is a well known shade tree, up to 60 feet high with rapid growth. The spreading branches form a large rounded crown. Propagated by seeds and marcots of woody branches. The Flame of the Forest does well in good well drained soil. During the flowering season, trees turn into a mass of red colour. When planted in an avenue, the sight is magnificent. Flowers are faintly scented, scarlet, one petal white with red spots.

Coral Tree, Dadap
Erythrina glauca
LEGUMINOSAE

An ornamental tree of tropical and subtropical regions, about 15 feet in height, with long erect panicles of flowers, dark crimson, about 2 inches long, and in groups of three. Propagated normally from woody cuttings. Used as a shade tree.

A native of South America, this deci-
ious tree has small delicate fernlike
ves. Reaching 40 feet in height, it
ows luxuriously in a well drained soil
d full sun. When in full bloom the
hole tree is covered with clusters of lilac
ue flowers on bare branches. It is best
own in avenues on both sides of the
ad. Individually, it is quite impressive
a small garden. It is grown easily from
ds.

**Jacaranda,
Jambul Merak**
Jacaranda ovalifolia
BIGNONIACEAE

Greater Frangipanni, Cempaka

Plumeria obtusa

APOCYNACEAE

A robust, growing tree, is often branched, and partly deciduous at different times of the year. A native of Tropical America, reaching a height of 20 to 30 feet, it needs a well drained soil and a sunny position. The flowers are large and fragrant, white coloured with a yellow centre. Flowers of various shades of colours are also found locally. It is propagated by marcots and cuttings.

Yellow Flame, Batai, Batai Laut

Peltophorum pterocarpum

LEGUMINOSAE

A medium size deciduous tree, up to 50 feet in height from Indo China, Malaysia to Australia. Yellow flame grows quickly, thus is seen everywhere—in waste lands, roadside and any open space. The spreading branches form a nice crown. Young trees will flower in 2–3 years. It is used for screening and shade. Propagated by seeds. The flowers are slightly fragrant, bright yellow in close erect branches. After flowering, the brown pods are persistent on the tree for some time and can look nice, having an ornamental effect.

Tembusu, Semesu
Fagraea fragrans
LOGANIACEAE

Distributed in the regions of Tenasserim, Lower Thailand and Sumatra, this is a tall ornamental tree, evergreen, reaching 100 feet in height, with profuse leaf growth. Flowering is seasonal and masses of fragrant creamy white flowers are seen covering the whole tree. Very useful as a tall screening plant, it grows well in heavy clay soil and is propagated by seeds and marcots.

Sea Hibiscus, Bebaru
Hibiscus tiliaceus
MALVACEAE

A native of Malaysia, it is a low spreading branched tree, evergreen and up to.40 feet in height with downy twigs. The flowers are bright yellow with maroon eyes. Propagated by seeds.

Vegetable Humming Bird, Sesban, Kacang Turi

Sesbania grandiflora

LEGUMINOSAE

A native of North East Asia, the Sesban is a small evergreen tree, 15–30 feet high. The tree does not grow vigorously, it has rather weak branches and leaves are scanty. The flowers are cream white or magenta pink. Propagated by seeds.

Potato Tree
Solanum wrightii
SOLANACEAE

A native of Brazil, it grows quickly into a bushy tree of 15 feet in height. Grown for its ornamental purpose, the flowers are violet changing to white when old. It requires a rich soil for good growth. Suited for planting singly. The leaves are large, lobed and prickly. Propagated by seeds.

Angsana, Sena
Pterocarpus indicus
LEGUMINOSAE

A very large deciduous tree, up to 100 feet high, having a dome shaped crown, is a useful shade tree. A native of Malaysia, it flowers seasonally in flushes of yellow and at the same time produces a nice scent. When they are planted in avenues, during the flowering season the roads can be littered yellow. Angsana grows very rapidly from woody cuttings of 4 to 6 feet in length.

A small branched, evergreen or partly deciduous ornamental tree, reaching 20 feet high. It is easy to grow. It requires a well drained soil and a sunny place. Propagated by marcots and cuttings. The flowers are fragrant, pink with a broad yellow centre.

**Temple Tree,
Temple Flower,
Common Frangipanni**
Plumeria acuminata
APOCYNACEAE

Mexican Lilac
Gliricidia sepium
LEGUMINOSAE

Mexican Lilac grows easily without much maintenance. As a shade tree, it is deciduous at times. It grows up to 30 feet high but the straggling branches are weak. The flowers are pinkish lilac, in season, the clusters cover bare branches, forming a very impressive small tree. The woody stem cuttings root readily and propagation is mainly by this means, also by seeds.

**Rose of India,
Crepe Flower,
Bungor**
Lagerstroemia flos-reginae
LYTHRACEAE

A deciduous tree with dense bushy growth, forming a nice rounded crown, not more than 50 feet high in the open. A native of India to Australia, the young trees require good soil for rapid growth. Marcotting is the more common means of propagation as it roots easily though we can propagate by seeds and cuttings. Flowering is seasonal. The flowers are in flushes, mauve pink to purple lilac. Commonly used as a shade tree even in small gardens, they are nice also in avenues.

An evergreen monopodial tree, grows to a height of 60 feet. A native from Himalayas to Malaysia, its young leaves are attractive, brilliant red in colour. Grows very slowly when young. At maturity it is a graceful looking tree, symmetrical to cone shape, becoming more rounded in outline when the tree grows older. An ornamental avenue tree, also used for screening. The flowers are large, white with yellow stamens and fragrant.

Ceylon Ironwood Tree, Penaga, Lenggapus
Mesua ferrea
GUTTIFERAE

African Tulip Tree
Spathodea campanulata
BIGNONIACEAE

A free flowering tree 70 feet high, evergreen with a good dense foliage. A native of Tropical West Africa. Serves as a useful tall screen. It requires good soil conditions for quick growth. Seeds and root-suckers are its common means of propagation. The flowers are large and of orange red colour.

A Season of Life

I look at you and see unfolding
the grace that is in this world:
At birth you are tiny perfection,
curled, half-wakening;
But soon the beauty you have become
enthrals me,
as you entwine with other boughs
and spend your honeyed season.
When at last your glory fades
and the sun's rays no longer dazzle
on your radiance;
Then quietly you give of yourself,
knowing, that through another,
your season of splendour will return.

RITA MONK

Ornamental Shrubs

Ornamental Shrubs

WOODY plants of moderate size are classified as shrubs. These plants are about 3 to 10 feet in height and are strong enough to stand by themselves without any support. Some of the taller shrubs can be called small trees. Shrubs are mainly planted in groups. When planted in pots they become restricted in size and can be even considered as pot plants; for example Bougainvillea and Mussaenda.

Shrubs like trees have different uses, depending on their habit and leaf colour. A number of bushy shrubs are attractive because of their variegated and brightly coloured leaves, their flowers being insignificant, for example Garden Croton (variegated leaves) and Poinsettia (brightly coloured leaves). Our national flower the Common Hibiscus *Hibiscus rosa sinensis* is a very good hedge plant which can stand constant trimming and produces large red flowers at all times. There are many hybrids which can be obtained by crossing with different species. Hybrids produce flowers of many shades and colours; white, yellow, orange, pink and red. They are also available in the single and multiple petal forms. Hibiscus grows well in light rich soil. It can also be planted as a pot plant.

Shrubs are also grown for their flowers. Either grown singly or in rows they can provide a lot of colours. An introduced plant, the Mussaenda a native of Philippines thrives very well in Malaysia. Over the past 5 to 10 years the small shrub has been very popular as they flower all the year round. Masses of white, pink or reddish bracts cover the entire plant.

Even in this small book there are forty species described under this class of plants i.e. ornamental shrubs. It is quite a task to select what to plant in one's garden, and to plant all of them the only suitable place is the botanical garden. Therefore in our selection we have to bear in mind their usage, and also whether the selected plants will thrive in our area and show their true colour. Some plants require a marked seasonal change in weather conditions e.g. a marked dry season before they bloom, some grow well only in the highlands, and others are indifferent.

Ornamental shrubs are mainly propagated by stem cuttings but some are grafted or marcotted. A few of them are propagated by seeds which are produced freely. Well known examples are Peacock Flower *Caesalpinia pulcherrima* and Drooping Cassia *Cassia fruticosa*. Seeds are sown in plastic bags or pots. When seedlings reach a height of 12 to 18 inches they can be transplanted into the ground. The seedlings should be tied to a stake. The general maintenance is similar to that for trees. However, after each flush of flowering the shrubs can be pruned to induce further flowering. At the same time pruning gives one a chance to train the shrub to a desirable shape.

Angel's Trumpet
Randia macrantha
RUBIACEAE

A native of Tropical Africa, it is a fine bush with dark green leaves. The flowers are in the shape of long trumpets, fragrant and white fading to creamy yellow. An ornamental plant, it is propagated by cuttings.

Hibiscus Shoe Flower, Bunga Raya, Bunga Pepulut

Hibiscus rosa-sinensis
MALVACEAE

Originated probably from China, it is a shrub with toothed leaves. Evergreen. The flowers are large, red, firm but scentless. Many hybrids have flowers ranging from white through yellow, and orange to scarlet and shades of pink, both single and double petals. Propagated by cuttings and budgrafting. Commonly used as a hedge, which can withstand cutting. It flowers continuously, even individually it looks nice. They can be planted in pots also.

Thunbergia
Thunbergia affinis
ACANTHACEAE

A bushy shrub of medium size from Tropical East Africa, with neat small foliage. Used in a mixed border or as a hedge. The flowers are large, deeply cup shaped, rich violet with a yellow throat. Propagated by cuttings.

Congea
Congea tomentosa
VERBENACEAE

A garden plant from Southern Thailand and Northern Malaysia. It is a rounded shrub with drooping hairy leaves. The flowers with white silvery bracts are arranged in a long inflorescence. It is a common garden plant, requiring good soil and initially when young, shade is necessary. Normally grown from seeds, but can also be propagated by woody cuttings.

Rose

Rosa spp.

ROSACEAE

There are 30–40 distinct species, although over 200 are described. Most of these species are indigenous to the temperate regions of the northern hemisphere. The habit of the rose is erect, climbing or trailing, often prickly, woody shrubs. The rose prefers cool conditions, but can be grown in the tropical lowlands. Flowers are solitary or in corymbs, they are of various colours and shades; and some are scented. Roses are mainly propagated by budgrafting and marcots.

Cape Honeysuckle
Tecomaria capensis
BIGNONIACEAE

A native of South Africa, this sm
shrub about 3 feet tall, needs a w
drained soil and full sun. Propagated
cuttings and seeds. Flowers are in a cl
cluster of bright orange on erect ste
above the leaves. Used as bedded pl
or border.

Yellow Bells
Stenolobium stans
BIGNONIACEAE

From Tropical America, it is a tall laxly shrub with compact erect branches of bell shaped yellow flowers. Normally it flushes every few weeks. Used as a border or bed of tall shrubs, along or mixed with other kinds. Propagated by woody cuttings and seeds.

45

Poinsettia
Euphorbia pulcherrima
EUPHORBIACEAE

A shrub from South Mexico. The short variety is 3–4 feet high with drooping bracts and flowering continuously. The tall variety flowers seasonally with bracts in horizontal groups. It has conspicuous red bracts forming a small colourful shrub in the garden.

Pagoda Flower
Clerodendron paniculatum
VERBENACEAE

A native of East Tropical Asia, the pagoda flower is a garden plant with large shining green, lobed leaves with a large compact pyramid of small, scarlet red flowers. Used in a mixed border, it is propagated by cuttings. Planted also for its massed effect, useful as a small garden shrub.

Bottle Brush
Callistemon lanceolata
MYRTACEA

A tree-like shrub introduced from New South Wales, it is sun-loving and drought resistant. The flowers are cylindrical spikes with masses of brilliant crimson brushlike stamens and dark yellow anthers. Bottle brush are attractive shrubs even individually in small gardens; they are propagated by marcots.

Bushy Cassia
Cassia biflora
LEGUMINOSAE

An ornamental shrub from Tropical America, reaching 12 feet in height with notched leaf tip. The flowers are rich yellow in a short terminal cluster. The plants produce bright flushes of yellow colours in the garden and flower consistently for months. They are useful plants for the small garden and easily grown from seeds.

Powder Puff, Calliandra
Calliandra surinamensis
LEGUMINOSAE

The Calliandra is a low spreading shrub or woody climber. It has a beautiful rounded shape with sprawling branches, its pinnate leaves in forked pairs. The flowers are pink, brushlike flower heads, with long silky stamens, reddish in the upper part and white below. Originated in Tropical America and India, it is grown from seeds and also by cuttings. The Calliandra grown in rows form a very attractive low screen.

Gardenia, Cape Jasmine
Gardenia florida
RUBIACEAE

An evergreen garden shrub, bushy habit with small shining dark gree leaves. Propagated by woody cutting The flowers are fragrant, large and pu white. It is a common garden plant.

Yellow Oleander
Thevetia peruviana
APOCYNACEAE

Introduced from West Indies and Mexico, the Yellow Oleander is a bushy shrub, sometimes becoming a treelet. Needs a sandy soil for good growth. The yellow flowers are fragrant and funnel shaped. Grown from seeds and woody cuttings.

Javanese Ixora

Ixora javanica

RUBIACEAE

A tall shrub from Malaysia, with large leaves and large flowerheads, flowering under light shade. The flowers are red, pink or yellow. Propagated by marcots and cuttings, they can be used for hedges also.

Shrubby Simpoh, Simpoh Ayer
Dillenia suffruticosa
DILLENIACEAE

A large evergreen shrub from West Malaysia, up to 20 feet high with large cabbagy leaves. This is a very common wild plant growing by the roadsides, seldom grown as a garden plant. The flowers have yellow petals with pale cream stamens. Normally propagated by seeds.

Cat's Tail
Acalypha hispida
EUPHORBIACEAE

Originally from West Indies the Cat's Tail is a showy tropical shrub with hairy leaves. Grown from cuttings, it has long pendant-like spikes of bright red flowers resembling foxtail.

Philippine Violet
Barleria cristata
ACANTHACEAE

A native of India, this shrub is bushy, medium size with simple leaves, flowering after being pruned. Used as a border, a bedded plant and hedge. Flowers are mauve, tubular form. Propagated by cuttings.

Witches Tongue
Clerodendron macrosiphon
VERBENACEAE

A small bushy shrub with small leaves.
The white flowers form delicate shapes
with their long tubular and rounded
structure. They appear in large masses.
They are grown from seeds and are also
useful as pot plants. Also grown in large
pots.

Crepe Myrtle
Lagerstroemia indica
LYTHRACEAE

A native of China, the Crepe Myrtle is a tall shrub, of open branching and small leaves. Flowering at a low height, sometimes becoming a small tree in the hills. The pink or mauve flowers have crinkled petals in terminal clusters. Grown from marcots and cuttings.

Pink Morning Glory
Ipomoea carne
CONVOLVULACEA

A stout woody shrub and also can b
a climber if not pruned. A native c
South America, it requires a sunny posi
tion. The leaves have wavy margins an
the flowers are large, of very pale pin
colour. Propagated by woody cuttings.

Madagascar Periwinkle
Vinca rosea
APOCYNACEAE

A small tropical erect shrub, 2 feet high, grown in full sun and sandy soil. The flowers are pink or white, used for bedding or grown in pots. They can be raised from seeds.

Pink Kopsia
Kopsia fruticosa
APOCYNACEAE

A native of Burma, the Pink Kopsia is tall, bushy with simple leaves. Growth is not rapid but does well when given good treatment. Marcots and cuttings are the normal ways of propagation. The flowers are pink with crimson eye. An ornamental commonly grown in groups in gardens.

Terong Susu

Solanum mammosum

SOLANACEAE

A small shrub with prickles on the leaves. Introduced from Central Africa, the flowers are blue and small. The fruits are more attractive than the flowers. Fruits are orange coloured, smooth and conical in shape with rounded lobes at its base, fruit about 3 inches long. Grown as an ornamental fruit for flower arrangement. The plants are propagated by seeds.

Singapore Rhododendron, Sendudok
Melastoma malabathricum
MELASTOMACEAE

A shrub or treelet 12–15 feet high if left grown undisturbed. From Madagascar, India to Australia, it is evergreen and with rough hairy leaf-blades. The flowers are purple magenta with yellow stamens, flowering throughout the year. Grown from seeds. They are common as wayside shrubs and thrive well in wasteland. It is seldom grown as a garden plant.

Red Pentas
Pentas coccinea
RUBIACEAE

A dwarf to medium size bushy shrub from Tropical Africa preferring light shade. Roots need shade from other plants if exposed to full sun. The flowers are bright red and in small heads. Propagated by cuttings. They are also grown in pots as ornamental plants providing splashes of red colours.

Red Mussaenda   Originated from West Tropical Africa,
Mussaenda erythrophylla it is a scandent shrub, preferring a place
RUBIACEAE   not too fully exposed. The true flowers
are yellow with brightly coloured red
bracts. They are useful as ornamental
shrubs along road dividers.

Yellow Allamanda
Allamanda cathartica
APOCYNACEAE

This is a very common plant in Malaysia. An introduced sprawling shrub from Brazil with glossy green leaves. The attractive flowers are large and yellow and flowering is all the year round. The plant is easily propagated from stem cuttings.

Adenium
Adenium coetenium
APOCYNACEAE

A bushy shrub with fleshy branches was introduced from East Africa and Arabia. It grows up to 2–3 feet tall and thrives well in the ground where soil is very sandy or in a large pot. Requires full sun for full bloom. The crimson flowers are beautiful but not very lasting. The plant is normally propagated by cuttings.

Lantana, Tahi Ayam
Lantana sellowiana
VERBENACEAE

A creeping shrub from South America with small leaves requiring a well drained soil and full sun. The flowers are mauve and in a corymb. Cuttings and layering are two ways of propagating Lantana. Used as a border, over a low wall. It can be grown in a hanging basket, creating a beautiful effect in the house patio.

Coral Hibiscus
Hibiscus schizopetalus
MALVACEAE

Originated from Tropical Africa, this is a bush like the Garden Hibiscus but with dangling flowers on slender stalks, petals pinkish white with toothed and slashed edge. It is best grown fully exposed to the sun, with rich soil and regular watering. Grown as a hedge, it is propagated by cuttings.

Rose of Sharon
Changeable Rose Hibiscus
Hibiscus mutabilis

MALVACEAE

A native of China, it is a laxly branched evergreen shrub or treelet with downy leaves and twigs. Usually grown as a hedge, the colour of the large flowers changes with temperature from white to pink. The plant is propagated by woody cuttings.

Sandpaper Vine
Petrea volubilis
VERBENACEAE

A sprawling bush, if left unpruned, becomes a woody climber. It makes beautiful archways. From South America, the flowers are lilac in colour, in delicate sprays. Propagated by cuttings.

Virgin Tree, Aurorae, Buddha's Lamp
Mussaenda philippica
RUBIACEAE

A native of Philippines, it is a medium size bush requiring good soil. The bracts are white or pink with orange tubular flowers. Woody cuttings or marcots are its only means of propagation. They flower all the year round and can be pruned drastically and new flushes of growth produce lovely pink or creamish white flowers. It is a very popular garden shrub and can be grown as pot plants also.

Oleander
Nerium oleander
APOCYNACEAE

A native of the Mediterranean region, it is an ornamental shrub which thrives best in sandy soil. If grown in clay or other heavy soil, the beds must be very well drained. Normally propagated by cuttings and marcots, occasionally by seeds. The flowers are in shades of white, pink, deep pink and dark red. It is a common garden plant.

Indian Ixora
Ixora coccinea
RUBIACEAE

A bushy short shrub from India, the Indian Ixora has stalkless leaves with broad bases, flowering throughout the year. It is slow in growth, requires full sun and is propagated by marcots and cuttings. The flowers are red, yellow and pink in colour. Commonly grown as a hedge or individually as a garden plant.

Shrimp Plant
Beloperone guttata
ACANTHACEAE

Introduced from Mexico, this Shrimp Plant is a medium size shrub with numerous erect shoots. The flowers are small, white, in the form of teardrops between dull red bracts. Used as borders and pot plants too. Propagation is by division of old plants and stem cuttings.

Golden Dewdrop, Pigeon Berry

Duranta repens

VERBENACEAE

An evergreen shrub, 6–18 feet high, requiring a sunny place. Flowering is frequent with pale blue or white flowers and golden coloured berries. It is propagated by woody cuttings and seeds.

An evergreen shrub which grows to the size of a small tree, is a very common hedge plant in Malaysia although it was originally from Tropical America. The plant has fairly large leaves and flowers are produced seasonally. The flowers are fairly large and pale pink in colour. But the hairy reddish fruits like rambutans are very attractive. The seeds produce an edible red dye. Propagation is fastest from cuttings but seeds can also be used.

Anatto, Kesumba
Bixa orellana
BIXACEAE

Peacock Flower,
Gold Mohur, Poinciana,
Pride of Barbados
Caesalpinia pulcherrima
LEGUMINOSAE

The peacock flower is an evergreen bush growing up to a small tree 25 feet high. The plant is prickly with bipinnate mimosa-like leaves. Flowers are orange red with golden edged petals and long red stamens. A common garden shrub from West Indies and the Tropics, it is grown usually from seeds.

Purple Bignonia
Bignonia magnifica
BIGNONIACEAE

A native of South Brazil and Paraguay, it is a very vigorous shrub and can be trained as a climber. It needs full sun for vigorous growth and flowering. Propagation is by woody cuttings. The flowers are large, bellshaped, mauve pink and appear frequently in flushes.

Creamfruit
Roupellia grata
APOCYNACEAE

A free flowering bush from Tropical Africa with climbing habits if left unpruned. Flowers are white suffused crimson, large and scented. It is propagated by cuttings and marcots.

Chalice Vine
Solandra nitida
SOLANACEAE

An ornamental woody evergreen, erect or clambering shrub, from Mexico with leathery elliptic glossy leaves. The flowers are chalice-shaped, 10-inch long with corolla reflexed and frilled, yellow with purplish stripes. Propagated by marcots.

Tropical
Climbers

Tropical Climbers

IN the tropical forests, creepers, climbers and vines are well adapted with hooks on their stems, tendrils and twining shoots to wind round the stem of tall forest trees as their support to reach for sunlight. Many of these climbers grow vigorously, competing with the forest trees for survival. The wild species in the jungle thrive well even in dense shade. But the cultivated species perform well in full exposure to sunlight while retaining their character of vigorous growth.

Domesticated climbers can be used for different purposes, mainly for shade as pergolas and arches around the house and patio. A number of species of the more slender types are used as climbers on fencing or even as screens. Thunbergia *Thunbergia grandiflora* is a fast growing climber with large dark green leaves and producing a long hanging attractive inflorescence which consists of large beautiful white flowers. Thunbergia forms a solid screen and provides a lot of shade thus being particularly good for patios and pergolas. The Morning Glory *Ipomoea cairica* is very useful as a covering of wire netting screens e.g. fencing for tennis courts. The Morning Glory produces pale mauve flowers very freely which open during the morning. Another very successful climber in the gardens for fencing is Tristellateia which profusely produces small yellow flowers in a pyramidal shaped inflorescence all year round. The famous Gloriosa Lily *Gloriosa superba* is a slender climber grown for its beautiful unusual flower with twisted red and yellow petals which turn upwards.

Climbers like all other plants can be either propagated from seeds or by vegetative means, usually stem cuttings. In planting a climber one should remember to provide a strong support whether it be a pergola, arch or fence as they have to cope with the great weight of the plant when it is fully grown. Climbers are known to have relatively poor root system, as such the planting hole should be deep and well manured to encourage better root growth both to support the plant against wind, and also to supply the needs of the dense foliage. Once a new climber is planted either as a cutting or seedling, it should be temporarily supported and leaned against the permanent strong support. In the initial stage, one can help the climber to twine round the support or fence so as to get the desirable directions of the climber. Once the plant is established there will be a mass of foliage and it is necessary to prune off old flowering shoots or leaves to make the pergola look tidy.

Bleeding Heart
Clerodendron thomsonae
VERBENACEAE

A slender climber from West Africa, requiring very good drainage when planted in the ground. It does not grow to a large size in Malaysia. The flowers are small, have red corolla with swollen white calyx. Propagated by cuttings. They can be grown also as ornamental pot plants or as border plants.

Honolulu Creeper, Corallita
Antigonon leptopus
POLYGONACEAE

Introduced from Mexico, this vigorous free flowering climber has herbaceous stems with tendril-like ends on its inflorescence for climbing. The flowers are bright pink, sometimes white. Grown on fences, arbours, pergolas and used as a screen. Propagated by seeds and cuttings.

Thunbergia, Sky Flower, Bengal Trumpet
Thunbergia grandiflora
ACANTHACEAE

A large coarse climber with long hang-ing inflorescence of large white flowers. A native of India, it needs tall support. The leaves are large and dark green form-ing dense foliage, very effective as a screen and on pergolas for shade. It grows easily and vigorously.

Rangoon Creeper, Drunken Sailor, Akar Dani
Quisqualis indica
COMBRETACEAE

A vigorous scrambling shrub or climber of South East Asia. Opening flowers are white turning crimson pink, fragrant and in bunches. Grown on archways or pergolas.

Gloriosa Lily
Gloriosa superba
LILIACEAE

A magnificent herbaceous climb
from Tropical Africa and Asia havi
tendril-like leaf tips for climbing. Glo
osa Lily requires a good rich soil, goo
drainage and shade at the roots. Grov
from small underground tubers a
seeds, its flowers consist of six narro
crinkled edged red and yellow peta
Planted on trellis, useful as cut flowe

A free flowering climber of Malaysia and Australasia requiring support and full sun. Propagated by seeds and woody cuttings. Small yellow flowers are in a pyramidal sprays. Used for pergolas and fences. They produce a constant yellow mass of colour.

Tristellateia
Tristellateia australasiae
MALPHIGIACEAE

Railway Creeper
Ipomoea cairica
CONVOLVULACEAE

A twining herb, very common in Malaysia, establishing itself on railway embankments, roadside and other similar places. The leaf is cut into five pointed lobes. The flowers have a purplish tinge. Grown from seeds. They are particularly useful as a screen on a wire netting fence of tennis courts.

Jade Vine
Strongylodon macrobotrys
LEGUMINOSAE

A woody climber introduced from the Philippines. It thrives well in cooler tropical regions as found in Penang Hill and Cameron Highlands, also found growing in the lowlands. The unusual jade coloured flowers hang from the plant in long trusses up to 2 feet long. The flowers are 2 to 3 inches long, shaped like the bean flowers. The jade vine climber makes an ideal pergola plant and needs a strong support. The common method of propagation is by marcotting.

Orchids

Orchids

MALAYSIA has won fame among the orchid growing countries. This is mainly due to the hundreds of wild native species and also the large number of hybrids bred locally which have won international awards. Orchids are considered exotic to the temperate regions where most of the orchids are grown in hot houses. Because of the high cost in temperate regions, orchid growing as a hobby is for the rich, but in Malaysia, orchids such as the ubiquitous *Vanda Miss Joachim*, and Spider Orchid *Arachnis flos-aeris* thrive in almost every garden and are useful as cut flowers.

Most of the wild orchids from the jungle have small or short-lived flowers. They do not adapt well in the urban environment and as such are unsuitable for use as garden plants. Today thousands of hybrids are produced artificially by crossing different but related species. In addition, the introduction of new propagation techniques i.e. germination of orchid seeds in sterilized nutrient agar have stimulated and enlarged the orchid industry in this country. Nowadays orchid plants are readily available at costs within the reach of the average man. Many new large orchid farms have been established lately and these cater for local and also for the export market as cut flowers.

Orchids are generally divided into three categories i.e. terrestrial, climbing and epiphytic. Terrestrial or ground orchids are those plants which are grown in the ground like any other plants. A good example is the common purple Spathoglottis *Spathoglottis plicata*. The

can also be grown in pots with good free draining garden soil. The climbing orchids as the name suggests grow and climb on to wooden supports. These plants have stems which bear aerial roots which stick to the support but some of the roots however will also reach the ground especially those at the base of the stem. The most common orchid in this group is *Vanda Miss Joachim*. It has a straight cylindrical stem bearing pencil like leaves and also has long roots. The flowers are fairly large, rosy mauve in colour, with the side lobes of the lip orange in colour. Epiphytic orchids are plants which grow above the ground i.e. on trees or on rocks. They have short stems of limited growth and new shoots arise from the base of the old stem. Their stems are known as pseudobulbs as they are solid bulblike structures and not true bulbs. The wild epiphytic species are naturally adapted to shady areas. The common Pigeon Orchid *Dendrobium crumenatum* are found on trunks and branches of big trees. Their flowers are small and white but not lasting. Different epiphytes require different conditions: some perform well even exposed to the sun, some prefer moderate shade. These epiphytic orchids can be grown attached to a piece of wood, fern roots, or coconut husks just to simulate natural conditions. In general they grow well in hanging wooden baskets, or in pots with large holes. These baskets or pots are filled with pieces of bricks, fern roots, moss, or charcoal which can absorb water and give it slowly to the roots, at the same time promoting free aeration which is necessary for healthy growth.

A whole book can be devoted to orchids; in this book only ten species are described. This collection represents the three categories of orchids i.e. terrestrial, climbing and epiphytic. Some of these are wild species such as the Pigeon Orchid, and the Tiger or Giant Orchid *Grammatophyllum speciosum*. The Giant Orchid is one of the largest orchid plants growing wild on the crowns of tall trees, but because of its size in the garden, it is often planted on the ground. The inflorescence can be as tall as six feet and the large flowers are about 4 inches across, of dull yellow colour with brownish orange markings.

The other species described here are also common species and hybrids which are popular cut flowers in the market and these are *Vanda Tan Chay Yan, Oncidium Golden Shower* and *Aranda Wendy Scott*. Orchids like other plants are propagated from seeds and by vegetative means. Formerly vegetative means are mainly used, such as stem cuttings, division of pseudobulbs and lateral buds. But over the past ten years propagation by seeds has been very successful and popular. Nowadays, the latest technique is by tissue culture, which has yet to catch on in Malaysia. The future of this technique has potential in the orchid industry.

Oncidium Golden Shower
(*Oncidium sphacelatum* ×
Oncidium flexuosum)
ORCHIDACEAE

A vigorous free flowering plant with close pseudobulbs. The flowers are bright canary yellow with brown markings (stripes). It is propagated by division. It is a very popular pot plant found in every orchid lover's garden and also grown in large quantities in nurseries for the cut flower market.

A free flowering plant able to stand full sun. The leaves are less than quarter terete. The flowers last for 3 weeks with the lower flowers dropping first before the inflorescence can attain full bloom. Grown in pots and in the ground, propagation can be made by cuttings or side shoots of the plant.

Sapanara Ahmad Zahab
(*Holtumura Eric Holtum* ×
Renanthera James Storeii)
ORCHIDACEAE

Aranda Wendy Scott
(*Arachnis hookeriana*
× *Vanda Rothschildiana*)
ORCHIDACEAE

This is a very popular hybrid in Malaysia. It is grown commercially in large acreage as cut flowers to supply local and overseas market. Wendy Scott is grown on stakes in the ground, growing vigorously producing flowers very freely. This climbing orchid is easily propagated by stem cuttings.

Tiger Orchid, Giant Orchid
Grammatophyllum speciosum
ORCHIDACEAE

An epiphyte of Malaysian jungle, the Tiger or Giant Orchid is a large plant producing a succession of thick leafy shoots. When cultivated on ground, leafy shoots are more or less erect curving outwards. On a tree, the long leafy branches hang down and the inflorescence normally six feet tall grows upwards. The plant requires aeration for its roots. Propagated by division. The flowers are large, 10 cm wide and are of pale yellow with large dull orange brown spots (stripes). This is the biggest epiphyte orchid species known. They are not very commonly grown in the gardens as they flower once or twice a year.

A terrestrial leafy plant, base of stem swollen into pseudobulb bearing a few long rather narrow pleated stalked leaves. Spathoglottis requires a very well aerated soil, liquid manure when in active growth. Propagated by division. The flower is primrose yellow with purple on the edges of sepals and petals, lip yellow and rosy purple. Used as a bedded or pot plant.

Spathoglottis Primrose
(*Spathoglottis plicata* ×
Spathoglottis aureus)
ORCHIDACEAE

Vanda Varayuth
(Vanda Lenavat × Vanda Coerulea)
ORCHIDACEAE

An orchid, grown in hanging basket. The flowers are big and of purple colour. Propagation is by removing the side shoots. Partial shade is required.

Pigeon Orchid
Dendrobium crumenatum
ORCHIDACEAE

A wild epiphyte found commonly growing on trees and bushes in the jungle and gardens. A native of Burma, Malaysia and South China, the Pigeon Orchid flowers after a sudden drop in temperature caused by rainstorms. The flowers are white with yellow on the lip, fragrant but unfortunately lasting for a day only. The plant multiplies itself rapidly by pseudobulbs, and can easily be propagated by division.

Moon Orchid, Moth Orchid
Phalaenopsis amabilis
ORCHIDACEAE

An orchid of Malaysia and Sunda Island, normally grown on pieces of wood, bark or coconut husk, in partial shade. The flowers are in a beautiful spray, large white with almost round petals. Propagation is using side shoots taken from old plants. Moon orchid is a very popular orchid in Malaysia. Free flowering.

Vanda Tan Chay Yan
(Vanda Josephine van Brero ×
Vanda dearei)
ORCHIDACEAE

A vigorous climbing plant with semi terete leaves, deep and widely channelled. They are grown in pots in full sun with a little shade around the base. Grown from cuttings, it has rich peach coloured flowers in a spike. Vanda Tan Chay Yan is one of the finest Vanda hybrids raised in the tropics. Now it has become very common. Formerly, they were only in the hands of some collectors. They are grown in large numbers in nurseries as cut flowers.

Ascocenda Piswong
(*Vanda Diana Ogawa*
× *Ascocenda Meda Arnold*)
ORCHIDACEAE

An orchid plant with strap leaves requiring partial shade. Grown in hanging pots, it is very free flowering. The length of the flower spray is about 13 inches. The flower size is about 2 inches across and 1.8 inches vertical. The flowers last for 2 weeks on the plant. Ascocenda cannot take organic manure, thus nutrients can be supplied to the plants in foliar spray. Propagated by side shoots.

Vanda Diana
*(Vanda teres var alba ×
Vanda White Wings)*
ORCHIDACEAE

Vanda Diana is a very common climbing orchid growing on stakes from the
ground. It is grown from stem cuttings.
The flowers are large and pure white
colour with some yellow inside the base
of lip. The plants flower very freely when
grown in full sun. Grown for cut flowers.

Miscellaneous Plants

Miscellaneous Plants

PLANTS like man are very adaptable to the natural environment. Their habits and habitat can change. For example the Tiger Orchid in the wild state grows on the crown of tall trees but cultivated they thrive as a terrestrial plant. Bougainvilleas when grown in pots can be considered as pot plants. When grown on the ground, they behave as shrubs and can even twine and climb and thus also are called scandent shrubs. Plants can also be classified as annuals and perennials depending on their life span. Those that complete their life cycle within a year are called annuals and those that live for a number of years are perennials. Plant are also classified as herbaceous if they do not possess woody stems. So there is no end to the various types of classification. Therefore in this miscellaneous section plants are grouped as pot plants, herb and aquatics.

Pot plants as the name suggests are plants grown in pots, big or small and they can be annuals or perennials. In this section only those that produce fairly attractive flowers are described. These plants can also be grown as bedded plant in fairly large plots to produce masses of colour in the garden. These are the balsams *Impatiens balsamina*, sunflower *Helianthus annuus*, *Chrysanthemum morifolium*. Dahlias *Dahlia pinnata* and many others. Herbaceous plants consist mainly of the bulbs such as spider lily *Hymenocaullis caribaea*. Finally there are the aquatic plant which thrive in water. In small gardens these plants are usually grown in concrete tanks, whereas in larger gardens artificial ponds with a clay soil can be established. Concrete tanks of various shapes and sizes can be very attractive when placed among rockeries or when paved by grasses. The popular species are Indian Lotus *Nelumbium nelumbo* and water lily *Nymphaea lotus*.

Propagation of pot plants is similar to that of trees, shrubs and climbers but their maintenance programme is quite different and they need more care. As pot plants are grown in a limited amount of soil, it is essential to supply sufficient nutrients and water daily. As for perennial plants they can become root bound i.e. excess roots in limited space. Therefore they have to be repotted regularly and the roots have to be pruned and new soil has to be used. Also to maintain a desirable shape the plant has to be pruned periodically especially after flowering to induce further new flowers. After pruning, fertilizers can be incorporated into the soil. Bougainvillea responds very well to pruning and use of organic fertilizers of bone and blood meal to induce free flowering. Different species require different environments, treatments and maintenance practices. The herbaceous and aquatic plants are mainly propagated by division.

Rose Moss
Portulaca grandiflora
PORTULACACEAE

A succulent herb with simple leaves. A native of America, Rose Moss has bright dazzling purple flowers. When grown in beds, they form a complete mat of colour. They are useful as plants for road dividers or even on embankments.

A perennial with leafy stems. Introduced from South Sea Islands, requiring a partially shaded position and good soil. The flowers are in a spike, about one foot in length, with brilliant crimson spathes. Propagated by division of plantlets.

Red Shell Ginger
Alpinia purpurata
ZINGIBERACEAE

Canna

Canna orientalis

CANNACEAE

An erect perennial herb with leafy stems, from Central and South America. Canna requires a mixture of manure and compost. Normally propagated by rootstocks, sometimes from seeds. Flowers are of various colours, the common ones are bright red and yellow. They flower very freely thus provide a lot of colours when planted in beds. It is useful as a low screen.

Spathiphyllum
Spathiphyllum cannaefolium
ARACEAE

A leathery plant with thick dull black green, corrugated leaves tapering towards the base. The flower consists of thick fleshy spathe green outside white inside, with a long free cream spadix. Grown as a pot plant and for its flowers, it is propagated by division of clumps.

Anthurium
Anthurium andreanum
ARACEAE

Epiphytes requiring a very well drained soil and thrive best in a pot half filled with broken bricks and a layer of fibrous leaf mould on top. A little shade is required. The flowers have bright red or pink spathes. Grown for cut flowers, Anthurium can be propagated by cuttings of fleshy stem or seeds.

Lobster's Claw
Heliconia humilis
MUSACEAE

A native of Tropical America, the plant is 3–8 feet tall, evergreen and needs a rich loamy well drained soil. In subtropical places, a sandy soil is required. Grown from rhizomes, the flower consists of brilliant scarlet spathe in the shape of a lobster's claw tipped with green and yellow. Because of its bright colour and lasting character, it is a very useful specimen for flower arrangement.

Torch Ginger, Kantan
Phaeomeria speciosa
ZINGIBERACEAE

A large plant from Indonesia growing to 15 feet high. Requires plenty of moisture, good soil and light shade provided by nearby trees. Flower is a cone shaped head, crimson pink edged white. Grown for cut flowers as well as a spice for cooking curries.

**Sunflower,
Bunga Matahari**
Helianthus annuus
COMPOSITAE

An annual herbaceous plant from Western United States. The flowers are in a very large head, orange yellow in colour. Each flowering head is made up of hundreds of ray and disc florets which are packed tightly together. The inflorescence or flower head is always mistaken for a flower. Grown from seeds, the sunflower is used as a bedding or a pot plant.

Japanese Canna
Heliconia psittacorum
MUSACEAE

A perennial plant from South and Central America Japanese Canna needs a wet ground to grow strongly with plenty of humus and full sun. Propagated by rootstocks the flowers have bright orange bracts. The leaves as well as the inflorescence are useful for flower arrangement.

Transvaal Daisy, African Daisy
Gerbera jamesonii
COMPOSITAE

This common daisy is found in many local gardens, it is always flowering and a perennial herb. The flowers are 3 inches in diameter and of various shades of colours—red, pink, orange and yellow. The flower has a long stalk and commonly used for flower arrangement. The African daisy originated from Africa and it can easily be propagated by division.

Bird of Paradise
Strelitzia reginae
STRELITZIACEAE

This is an exotic plant to Malaysia and the neighbouring countries, it is a native of South Africa. The large bright orange coloured flowers resemble a bird on a long stalk. The flower stalk is fairly long rising above the leaves which are quite similar to those of canna and the Japanese canna. Plants can be propagated by division.

Dahlia, Bunga Sarang Tebuan
Dahlia pinnata
COMPOSITAE

A herbaceous annual from Mexico, dahlias require full sun, very good drainage and intensive manuring for good growth. The flowers are of many colours, brilliant yellow, white, orange, dark red, pink and purple. They can be grown in pots as well as in beds. The size of flowers vary from 2–8 inches in diameter. They are used as cut flowers.

Bougainvillea, Bunga Kertas
Bougainvillea spp.
NYCTAGINACEAE

A pot plant, perpetually flowering, single and multi bract forms are found. Requires good soil and is pruned after each flowering to enable new growth and to maintain its shape. Propagated by woody cuttings. The flower bracts are of various shades, ranging from bright purple, light purple, white, orange and red.

A herbaceous plant originally from China needs a very good drainage, occasional liquid manure and full sun. The flowers are of white and bright yellow colours with intermediate shades. Propagated by green cuttings and seeds. Grown for cut flowers.

Chrysanthemum, Kekwa
Chrysanthemum morifolium
COMPOSITAE

Herbaceous plant requiring plenty of light but thrives best without full exposure to sun. Begonias require good drainage and regular manuring. Propagated by leaf cuttings. Flowers are pink and in a cluster.

Begonia
Begonia maculata
BEGONIACEAE

Hydrangea, Bunga Tiga Bulan
Hydrangea macrophylla
SAXIFRAGACEAE

A herbaceous plant from China, requiring intensive manuring and light shade. Propagated from small green cuttings, it is grown as a pot plant and for cut flowers. Treatment of plant with aluminium sulphate in an acid soil can bring some pink flowers of hydrangea varieties to blue colour.

A common short herbaceous garden plant, it is grown in pots or in beds. Flowers are of various colours. The pink, white and mauve, single and multiple petal forms are available. They are grown from seeds.

Garden Balsam, Inai Ayam
Impatiens balsamina
BALSAMINIACEAE

Salvia
Salvia splendens
LABIATAE

Salvia is a temperate species but are introduced and thriving even in the tropical lowlands. It is a herbaceous plant lasting over a year or more. They grow well even as pot plants and form a nice border with their brilliant red flowers. Propagation is normally by seeds imported from overseas.

Sea Egg, Powder Puff
Haemanthus multiflorus
AMARYLLIDACEAE

This rather uncommon bulbous plant in this country has its origin from Africa. It is a beautiful plant producing a large head of inflorescence which is made up of hundreds of small red flowers to give it the look of a large powderpuff of 4 to 8 inches in diameter. The flowers are not very lasting ranging from 5 to 10 days. Mode of reproduction is vegetative —by means of bulb division.

ider Lily
menocaullis caribaea
ARYLLIDACEAE

pider lily is a very common bedded
at in gardens. It is a free flowering
ennial herb from South America, bul-
s, with sword shaped leaves. Grown
n bulbs. Used as a border or pot
at.

Red Lilies
Hippeastrum reticulatum
AMARYLLIDACEAE

A native of Brazil the bulbous plant
has a fleshy erect stalk of three or more
flowers. The leaves are strapshaped and
dark green with an ivory white midrib.
Grown from bulbs, the flowers are trum-
pet shaped, white veined pink. Grown
for cut flowers and as a pot plant.

145

Sea Daffodil
Pancratium zeylanicum
AMARYLLIDACEAE

A dwarf growing lily with white flowers which are short lived. Propagated by seeds and bulbils, this daffodil originates from Ceylon. Normally used in small beds and also as borders of larger beds.

Gladiolus
Gladiolus tristis
IRIDACEAE

This is a temperate species introduced to the tropics as such are doing better in the highlands, eg. Fraser's Hill and Cameron Highlands. There are many varieties of different colours, red yellow and orange. The flowers are arranged in long stalks as such are useful as cut flowers for arrangement. Plants produce corms, which are used for propagation.

Tuberose, Sundal Malam, Yok Chum
Polyanthus tuberosus
AMARYLLIDACEAE

An unattractive tuberous grass like plant but it produces a very long fragrant inflorescence up to 4 feet tall. The inflorescence consists of numerous white waxy flowers of 2" in length. They are very useful as cut flowers, in great demand during festive seasons. The white flowers are commonly dyed to various shades of colours by florists. Tuberose is a native of Mexico. Propagation is by means of stem division.

Water Hyacinth,
Keladi Bunting
Eichornia crassipes
PONTEDERIACEAE

A floating plant of South America with leaf stalks developed into bladders. The water hyacinth grows well in mud near surface of water. They multiply very rapidly by offset division and can cover the whole water surface of ponds, thus they become serious weeds. The flowers are delicate and of mauve colour.

Water lily, Telipok
Nymphaea lotus
NYMPHAEACEAE

An aquatic introduced from Egypt.
The leaves and flowers float on the water.
The flowers can be white, pink, yellow
or purple colour. Propagated from
rhizomes.

An aquatic grown in ponds and still
ters. Leafstalks of lotus stand high
ove the water. The plant requires at
st a foot of rich soil and well rotted
nure and a foot of water in depth.
opagation can be made from rhizomes,
grown from seeds. The flower petals
rose pink with yellow stamens.

**Sacred Lotus,
Telipok, Teratai**
Nelumbium nelumbo
NYMPHAEACEAE

Propagation, Planting and Maintenance

I. PROPAGATION

PLANTS reproduce vegetatively or sexually. One can multiply the number of plants by a large variety of methods; seed sowing, leaf and stem cuttings, and the division of plant clumps are most common and practical. However, specialized techniques have to be used when plants do not produce seeds or root easily, in which case budgrafting and marcotting of plants have to be practised. In the tropics with constant high temperature and humidity, no specialised equipment or propagator units are required. In general for successful propagation, consideration should be given to plant hygiene. Whenever possible, pots, seed boxes and cutting implements should be clean and perhaps the soil sterilized. In vegetative propagation, whether it be leaf or stem cuttings or grafting, it is essential that clean cuts are made with razor sharp secateurs or budding knives. Newly propagated materials such as cuttings should be kept under humid conditions. Successful plantlets or new plants are then transplanted into pots.

(1) SEED SOWING

This is a very simple procedure and usually instructions are given in the packet of seeds on sale. Seeds can be sown in pots, seed boxes or nursery beds. A general principle is to sow seeds to a depth about twice the length or diameter of the seed. Most fine seeds are thinly broadcast on the soil mixture and they are then covered lightly with another layer of soil. Care should be taken that watering is done with a can fitted with a fine rose to prevent seeds being washed away. In the case of a seed box or pot, a sheet of clear glass can be placed on top, but make sure the glass is well above the soil. Seedlings should not be placed in direct sun. Once they are 2–3 inches high they can be transplanted into bigger pots (see plate 1).

Plate 1.   A seed box with seedlings ready for transplanting.

Plate 2.   Orchid seedlings growing on nutrient agar in a flask.

(2) GERMINATION OF ORCHID SEEDS

Orchid seeds are very tiny and the embryos are not fully developed, therefore special care is necessary to ensure success in their germination. These minute seeds must be provided with special nutrient for their nourishment when they are undergoing germination, unlike other seeds such as sunflower seeds which have a large food reserve. A technique has been designed to germinate orchid seeds on sterilized nutrient agar. Sterilized seeds are sown thinly on nutrient agar in bottles or conical flasks. After germination, the seedlings grow quite vigorously while in the flask. Once they have grown to height of an inch they are ready for transplanting to community pots (see plate 2). Later each seedling is again transplanted into an individual pot.

(3) STEM AND LEAF CUTTINGS

Stem cuttings are obtained by cutting off the shoots of the plant. These are soft wood cuttings. A clean cut is made 4–6 inches below the tip of the shoot or other part of the stem. Hard wood cuttings are made from those of mature wood. In Hibiscus and Crotons, stems about the size of a pencil are chosen. Pieces of stems 6–12 inches long can be cut with the base cut at an angle (see plate 3). The leaves are removed before the cutting is placed in the rooting medium. The cut ends of the stem are often moistened and dipped in rooting or hormone powder before inserting in the rooting medium. In the case of orchids such as the common *Vanda Miss Joachim* and *Vanda Tan Chay Yan*, a cutting of 1 to 2 feet is made from the mature shoot (see plate 4). The stem cuttings possessing aerial roots are planted in a pot or on the ground and tied to stakes.

B — Stem cutting with end cut at an angle.

C — A successfully rooted stem cutting ready for planting.

Plate 3. Stem cuttings:
A — Leaves are removed from a selected Croton cutting.

Plate 4. A Stem Cutting from Vanda Orchid

Plate 5. Leaf Cuttings:
A — An Iron Cross
Begonia leaf is cut.

B — Cut pieces of leaves are placed in a pot
with sand as a rooting medium.

For leaf cuttings, a vigorous healthy plant is selected. In Pepperomia, the leaf is cut off from the plant at the base of the petiole and inserted into the rooting medium. Another technique is to cut up the leaf into pieces as shown (plate 5). Fresh, uninjured leaf of Iron Cross (*Begonia masoniana*) is cut up into small pieces, about the size of a postage stamp. The pieces are then placed on moist medium with the coloured side facing upwards. The medium must be just moist; if it is too wet, they will rot and when it is too dry, they will shrivel.

A simple and effective propagator can be easily made as follows: A box or pot of 4 to 6 inches deep with holes at the bottom is used. The box or pot is filled at the bottom with a layer of stones, which are then covered with sieved, cleaned river sand (the rooting medium commonly used) to a depth of 4 inches.

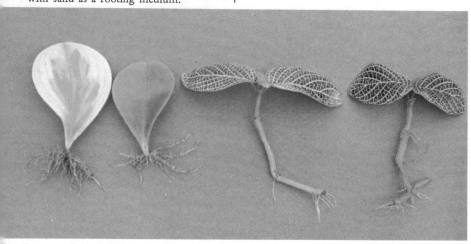

— Pepperomia leaf cuttings cut from base of petiole. Right — herbaceous stem cuttings of Fittonia.

157

This pot is then ready to receive the cuttings. After the cuttings have been inserted, the pot is covered with a polythene bag or the whole pot and cuttings are placed in the bag which is then sealed on top (see plate 6). The reason for this is to keep the atmosphere moist and reduce water loss from the leaves so that the leaves and stem will remain fresh and turgid while rooting takes place.

Plate 6. Plant propagator units:
A — A simple propagator: A pot with stem cutting is enclosed in a polythene bag.

B — A large commercial propagator unit, with concrete tanks which are fitted with an automatic sprinkling system to keep the cuttings moist all the time.

(4) DIVISION

Plants which produce suckers, rhizomes, bulbs and tillers can be easily multiplied by simple division from the clump of mother plants. This form of propagation is very simple and common among the orchids with pseudobulbs such as Dendrobiums and other plants such as Dracaena and Sansevieria. The procedures are simple, in the case of orchids. A healthy plant with a young or new pseudobulb from the base of an old one is selected. A cut is made in the new pseudobulb and 3 weeks after this, when new roots have been produced the pseupobulb can then be entirely severed and repotted immediately (see plate 7). In case of a potted plant, the compost or soil should be thoroughly wet before the clump is separated. A sharp knife is used to cut through the stem and root portions (see plate 8). Each portion should have many roots attached. The portion is then potted.

Plate 7. Division of Pseudobulbs: New pseudobulb is removed from the parent plant.

Plate 8. Division of Clumps: A new shoot of Sansieviera clump is removed from the main clump.

(5) MARCOTTING OR AIR LAYERING

A number of plants do not root readily and are not propagated by stem or leaf cuttings, for example Amherstia. A special method of plant propagation known as marcotting or air layering is practised. By this method the plantlets continue to get nourishment from the parent while they are producing their own roots. In marcotting, a straight branch about 2 feet long with a diameter of a pencil or larger can be chosen. Two incisions are made right round the branch, the distance between two incisions being twice or thrice the diameter of the branch. The bark between the two incisions is completely removed and then the cambium is scraped (see plate 9A). The barkless band is then covered with a clay mixture made to a ball of about 3 inches in diameter. The ball of clay mixture is then covered with polythene sheet or coconut fibres. Then it is tied above and below the ball (see plate 9C). In the case of a polythene cover, there is no need to water the marcot but when coconut fibre is used, watering is necessary. After 1 to 3 months, roots can be found in the clay mixture. When sufficient roots are produced, the branch is cut off below the marcot (see plate 9C). The marcot is then potted after the removal of the polythene covering, taking care not to disturb the root-filled ball of clay. The potted marcot is put in a sheltered place. After the marcot is fully established, it can be planted in the field.

B — The barkless band is covered with a clay mixture and polythene sheet.

Plate 9. Marcotting:
A — The bark between the two incisions is completely removed and cambium is scraped.

C — A Mussaenda marcot is ready to be cut from the parent plant.

II. PLANTING

(1) RAISING SEEDLINGS IN SEED BOXES

Seeds are usually not planted in a place where they are to be grown permanently. It is a normal practice to raise plants from seedlings in a nursery and then transplant them at a later stage in the garden. This is necessary because seedlings need extra care. When they become more hardy they can withstand field conditions better.

In raising seedlings, seeds are usually sown in a seed box. A box of 18 inches square and 4 inches deep can be made for planting seedlings. An alternative is to use a 4-inch deep round pot of 18 inches diameter. The box or pot is filled with a mixture containing 2 parts of garden or jungle soil, 1 part of decomposed compost and 1 part of sand. The mixture is gently made firm and level with the aid of a flat piece of wood. The flower seeds for example Balsam are scattered on the surface of the soil or sown in rows. After sowing, the seeds are covered with finely sieved soil to a depth of approximately twice the diameter of the seeds. Then they are watered using a can with a fine rose.

When seedlings become large enough to handle (2–3 inches tall), they are often "pricked out" into individual pots, plastic bags or into beds (see plate 10). With the aid of a stick, a hole is made in the soil of the pot or bed. The seedling is placed into the hole making sure that the main root is not bent. The hole is then filled with soil and the soil around the seedling is pressed to make it firm. The soil around the seedling is covered with mulch or dry leaves and the seedling is watered. The seedlings in pots or beds should be kept under shade for a few days till new leaves are produced. The transplanting of seedlings is best done in the evenings or on a dull day.

Plate 10.   Seedlings are raised in polythene bags.

(2) ESTABLISHING AN ORNAMENTAL TREE IN THE GARDEN

Planting an ornamental tree in the garden is similar to planting a fruit tree. A special planting hole is necessary, whether plants are grown from a seedling, a bud-grafted plant or a marcot. A hole of $3' \times 3' \times 2'$ is dug. If the soil is poor, it is advisable to replace it with garden soil. A kerosene tin filled to the top with rotted cowdung or chicken dung is mixed with the garden soil and a few ounces of fertilizer such as rock phosphate can be included and the hole is then filled. The plant in the pot or bag is first watered a few hours before planting in the garden. A small hole is then dug in the prepared planting area deep enough to take the bagged plant. The plant is removed from the pot or bag with care. In the case of the plastic bag, a cut is made and the plant is lifted out carefully and placed erect in the hole. The hole is filled with soil and the soil compacted. The plant is tied to a stake. The soil is covered with mulch or well rotted leaves. The plant is watered and shade is provided by sticking two or three coconut fronds a foot away from the stem (see figure 1).

The newly planted tree is watered daily if there is no rain. When the tree is established, with the production of a few new leaves, the shade can be removed.

III. MAINTENANCE

Ornamental plants whether they be trees, shrubs climbers or pot plants have to be maintained carefully after planting so that the plants can look their best and the gardener can be proud of his plants. This is the basic aim of every gardener. It is very disappointing to see in many private gardens, plants which are weak looking and choked with weeds all over the place, in contrast to most Botanic Gardens where the plants are growing vigorously and flowering freely due to a higher standard of maintenance. Like all living things one must provide them with water, food and a favourable environment to grow. In the same manner plants have to be watered, given manure as nutrients, be pruned by removing the unwanted parts to induce new growth and produce a desirable shape. One must observe a certain degree of hygiene to keep the plants and their surroundings clean, also to protect them against pests. Different plants have their special requirements and also their preferences. In this section, there is no room to cater for individual preferences, so only the general principles of watering, manuring, re-potting, pruning and protection of plants against pests are discussed.

(1) WATERING

Watering a plant may sound such a simple job and yet many make mistakes in this procedure. In principle plants should be watered adequately as and when they need it, and not just at regular intervals. In watering ground plants sufficient water must be given to penetrate to the root level and below. Potted plants require more moisture than those on the ground because of the restricted amount of water the soil can hold. A pot has to be watered once the surface begins to dry. Normally pot plants in the open will require watering twice a day, morning and evening. Care must be taken that water reaches the roots and not just wet the foliage. In watering newly sown seed boxes or young seedlings care must be taken not to water them roughly with a hose. A can with a fine rose has to be used and the seedlings are to be watered gently to prevent the seeds or seedlings from being washed away.

Orchids raised in baskets or pots containing only broken bricks and charcoal require watering twice a day, morning and evening unless it rains. Those grown in the shade and those grown in fibre require watering once every second day

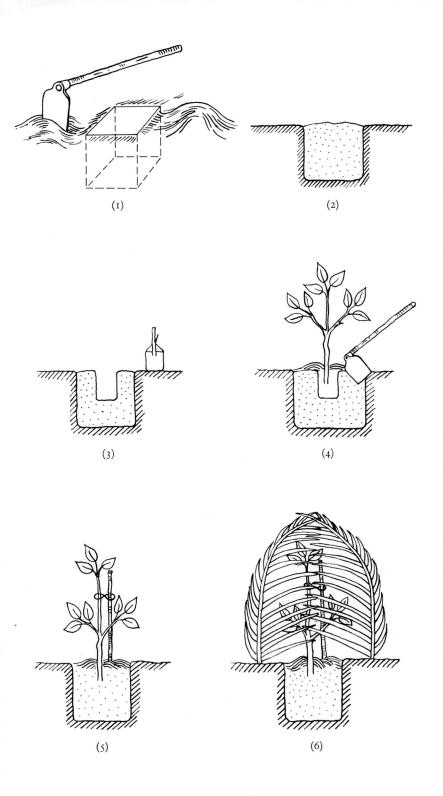

Figure 1. Stages in planting seedlings:
(1) A planting hole is dug.
(2) Hole is filled with soil mixture.
(3) Small hole is dug in the planting area.
(4) Seedling is lowered into hole.
(5) Seedling is tied to a stake.
(6) Seedling is shaded.

(2) MANURING

In the hot tropics the plants grow continuously therefore they require nutrients in large amounts. Fertilizers can be of two types, organic and inorganic, a combination being often preferable. Organic manures when added to soil help to maintain the soil in a friable condition. Commercial inorganic fertilizers are available in various forms—liquids, crystals or granules and pellets. Instructions given in the container have to be followed. Care must be taken not to apply excessive amounts which will kill the plants. In general fertilizers are applied around the root region of the plant but not too close to the stem. Fertilizers for pot plants can be incorporated into the soil with a fork once every 3 or 4 weeks after weeding. Similarly trees can be treated in the same manner. However, the manuring of orchids is quite different especially for the Dendrobiums which are potted in the open and sterile medium of broken bricks and charcoal. It is necessary to supply these plants with nutrients. The best method is to apply a liquid manure which has been diluted. Small quantities are applied at regular intervals, once or twice a week. The common manure for orchids are urine, fresh fish water, cattle dung, and other commercial preparations.

(3) REPOTTING

After planting, sooner or later the roots of the plant in a pot will fill up all the available space and the plant is described as rootbound. Growth slows down or stops completely. Once the plant has reached this condition it has to be repotted and this occurs in the perennial plants, such as Bougainvillea. In this case the plant is taken out of the pot with care. The excessive root growth especially the old and decayed roots, have to be removed with a secateur, and also the old soil is removed. The plant after root pruning is again planted into another pot with fresh soil compos[t]. Normally the repotted plant is prune[d] and new flushes of leaves and flowe[rs] will follow.

(4) PRUNING

The essence of pruning is to remov[e] old and diseased parts of the pla[nt] to induce new growth of leaves an[d] flowers, and simultaneously to train th[e] plant into a desirable shape. During th[e] initial stage of growth, formative prun[n]ing is practised to produce the desire[d] shape at maturity. If this is neglected, [it] is difficult to correct later. In a shade tre[e] for example, it is essential to have a clea[n] trunk to a height of 6 feet or more befor[e] any branching is allowed. Side branch[es] on the young tree must be removed u[p] to the desired height. If a tree is plante[d] for a screen, then the treatment give[n] will be different. In this case side branch[es] are encouraged or even induced.

An ornamental shrub or pot pla[nt] should also undergo formative prunin[g] at the early stages of growth. Once [a] mature plant is in good shape with th[e] desirable framework, the routine prunin[g] is carried out at the end of each flowerin[g] period, during which the old twig[s] bearing the remains of flowers are r[e]moved to induce new shoot formatio[n] which will in turn bear the new flower[s] Therefore, subsequent pruning is to e[n]sure the production of flowers as well [as] to remove any diseased or undesirab[le] shoot or branch.

(5) WEEDING

Weeds are referred to as plants in th[e] wrong place, for example grasses grow[]ing in flower beds are weeds. Weeds ha[ve] to be removed for a number of reason[s] they compete with the plants for nut[ri]ents and water; they shade them; a[nd] are very untidy amongst the flowe[rs] Therefore weeds have to be controll[ed] by various means. The simplest is ha[nd] weeding; by this it means the weeds a[re]

individually pulled out from the surroundings of the flowering plants. Weeds
can also be removed with the aid of a
fork. In the case of a shrub or tree, the
changkol is often used, to remove weeds
round the tree. Chemical weed killers
can be used but care must be taken that
the weedicide is sprayed only on the
weeds and not on the flowering plant.
Instructions are always given outside the
container. Most of the weedicides are
poisonous, therefore we have to handle
them with great caution.

d) PESTS AND DISEASE CONTROL

All plants are susceptible to attack by
insects, fungi and viruses causing diseases
or mere mechanical damage, for instance
the garden snails and grasshoppers can
cause great damage especially to young
seedlings by eating off the leaves and
stems. Fungi, bacteria and viruses cause
serious diseases in plants which may des-
troy the whole crop of flowers resulting
in total loss and disappointment. Therefore all pests and diseases have to be
controlled by various means available.
In the case of snails, pellets which kill the
snails by contact are sold commercially.
Snail pellets can be placed on the ground
round the base of plants. Insecticides
and fungicides in the form of dusts and
solutions can be used to protect the plants;
instructions are always given in the con-
tainers and must be followed strictly.

In orchids the main pests are insects
such as thrips, beetles and scale insects.
A regular weekly spray with tuba root
(Derris) or a DDT emulsion can get rid
of thrips. Gammexane is good for the
control of beetles.

Bibliography for Further Readings

Corners, E.J.H. (1952): *Wayside Trees of Malaya.* 2 vol. Govt. Printing Office, Singapore.

Corners, E.J.H. & Watanabe (1969): *Illustrated Guide to Tropical Plants.* Hirokawa Publishing Company Inc. Tokyo, Japan.

Davidson, W. (1969): *Woman's Own Book of House Plants.* The Hamlyn Publishing Group Ltd., London.

Henderson, M.R. (1961): *Common Malayan Wild Flowers.* Jarroed & Sons Ltd., Norwich. London.

Henderson, M.R. & Addison, G.H. (1956): *Malayan Orchid Hybrids.* Govt. Printing Office, Singapore.

Holtum, R.E. (1953): *Gardening in the Lowlands of Malaya.* Straits Times Press Ltd., Singapore.

Holtum, R.E. (1953): *Flora of Malaya Vol. 1—Orchids.* Govt. Printing Office, Singapore.

Holtum, R.E. (1954): *Plant Life in Malaya.* Lowe and Brydone (Printers) Ltd., London N.W. 10.

Graf, A.B. (1968): *Exotica 3, pictorial cyclopedia of exotic plants. Guide to care of plants indoors.* Roehrs Co. Inc. N.J. 07073 USA.

Keng, H. (1969): *Orders and Families of Malayan Seed Plants.* Univ. of Malaya Press, Singapore.

Stirling, M. (1974): *Tropical Flowers and Plants.* Paul Hamlyn Pty. Ltd., NSW 2099.

Index to Common Names

Index to Botanical Names